Cont

Mysterious creatures 2

North America 10

South America 20

Africa 26

Europe 32

Asia 36

Glossary 46

Index 47

Mysterious creatures

For centuries, mysterious ape-like creatures have been reported around the world. Some have been seen in mountain ranges, others in thick forests. Some even lurk in swamps. In these wild places, they mostly remain hidden from view. But now and then, somebody spots one. However, no one has found definitive proof that these creatures exist. Many scientists say they are simply not real.

The creatures seem to look different in different countries, but they do have many things in common. Most are reported to be giant, covered in hair and armed with sharp teeth. Some say they look like tall gorillas; others describe them as huge, hairy humans. Most are fast-moving and super-strong. Some eat berries, while others feed on sheep and goats. Thankfully, attacks on humans are rare.

Around the world

Different countries have different names for the creature. This is what it is called around the world:

Europe: Am Fear Liath Mor (say: *Arm-fer-lee-mo-er*) in Scotland, UK; Brenin Llwyd (say: *Bre-nin-flowe-wid*) in Wales, UK

North America: Bigfoot in the USA; Sasquatch in Canada

Asia: Yeti or Abominable Snowman in Nepal and Tibet; Yeren in China

South America: Mapinguari (say: *Map-ping-wah-ri*) in Brazil; Ucumar (say: *U-qu-mer*) in Chile and Argentina

Africa: Ngoloko (say: *Ing-go-loco*) in Tanzania; Chemosit (say: *Kee-mo-sit*) in Kenya

My Yeti journal

I saw my first Yeti when I was eight years old. I was walking with my mother in a mountain forest. It was a crisp winter's day and the snowy ground crunched loudly beneath our feet.

Ben Hubbard

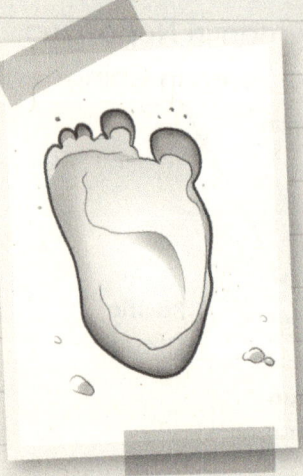

But then, we found a massive footprint in the snow before us. It was twice as long as a human foot, had five toes, and left a deep imprint. Whatever made it must have been large and heavy.

Suddenly, my mother grabbed my hand and froze. Ahead, half-hidden by the trees, was a creature covered in hair. Taller than a football goal, it had a head like a coconut, and long arms that hung below its knees.

"A Yeti," my mother gasped.

It stood there staring at us, as we stared back. Its breath looked like smoke in the cold air. Then, without a sound, it turned and sped away. Within seconds, it had raced out of sight, jumping over boulders and ducking branches.

Our **encounter** had lasted less than a minute. But my interest with the Yeti has remained.

Since then, I've travelled the world trying to find and film other creatures just like it. The creatures are known by lots of names, such as Bigfoot, Sasquatch and the Abominable Snowman. I mostly call them "Yetis". But no one has proven they exist. Until now ...

Anatomy of a Yeti

What does a Yeti look like? In the Himalayas it is said to be covered in white, grey, brown, beige, red or black hair. In North America, the Sasquatch and Bigfoot have black, red, beige or brown hair. Almost all of them have huge feet.

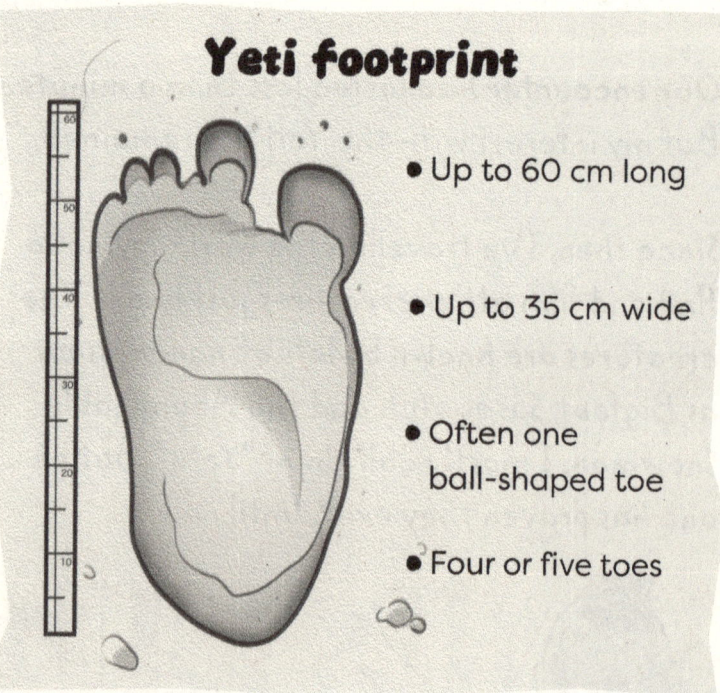

Yeti footprint

- Up to 60 cm long
- Up to 35 cm wide
- Often one ball-shaped toe
- Four or five toes

This footprint is based on one found in the Himalayas in 1951, by mountaineer Eric Shipton.

This is how a typical creature looks:

A Yeti

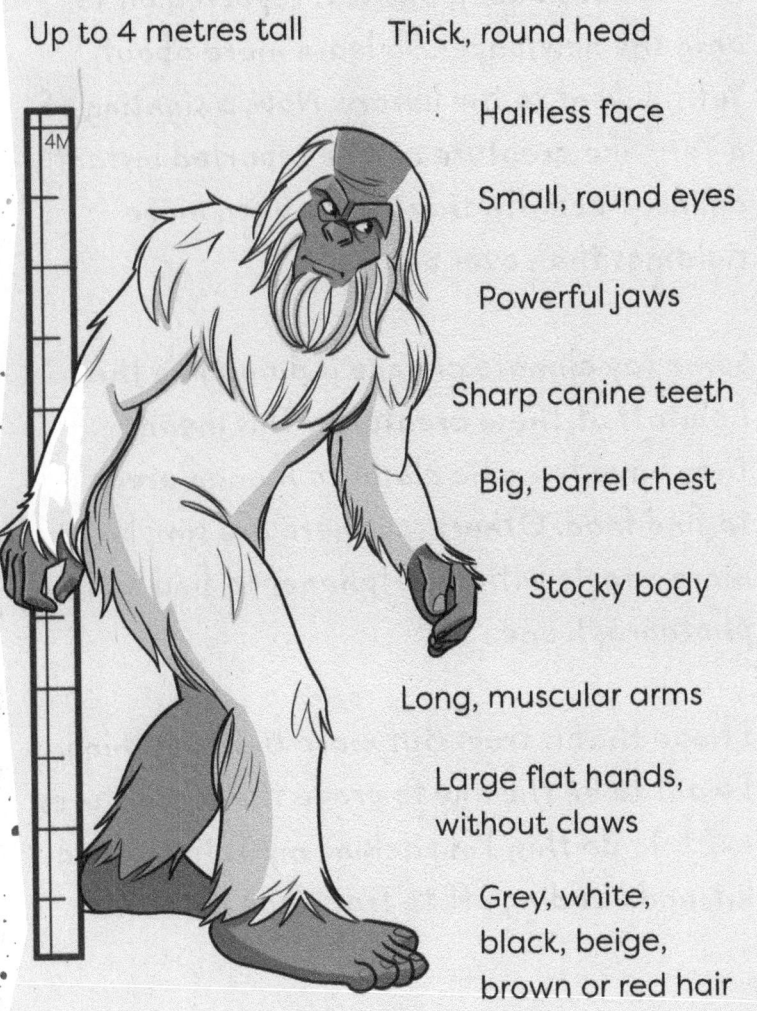

Up to 4 metres tall

Thick, round head

Hairless face

Small, round eyes

Powerful jaws

Sharp canine teeth

Big, barrel chest

Stocky body

Long, muscular arms

Large flat hands, without claws

Grey, white, black, beige, brown or red hair

Yeti hunting

When I was a child, Yeti sightings seemed rare. Occasionally, one was reported on TV or in the newspaper. To learn more about Yetis, I went to the library. Now, a sighting of a Yeti-like creature can be reported instantly online. Recently, there have been more sightings than ever before.

Some say climate change is damaging the habitats of these creatures. This means they have to come closer to human areas to find food. Others say there are simply more people with smartphones to find and photograph one.

I hope that is true. But more than anything, I want to be the one to prove these creatures exist. To do this, I'm packing my Yeti-hunting kit, and heading off to track one down.

Yeti-hunting kit

- Digital camera and spare batteries
- Solar-powered chargers for phone and camera
- Mosquito repellent
- Bear spray
- Maps of each country, wrapped in plastic
- Plastic compass
- Head torch
- First aid kit
- Knife for sharpening sticks, gutting fish and cutting bandages
- Emergency rations
- Waterproof matches and a plastic lighter
- Two-metre-long piece of lightweight rope
- Foldable shovel
- Binoculars with night vision

North America

There's been a sighting of the Sasquatch in British Columbia, Canada.

Although it's Christmas, I jumped on the first flight here. I've hired a car and am heading for the village of Silverton.

My local **contact** says the Sasquatch tracks are still visible in the snow. This is very exciting news!

SASQUATCH

Height:	2–4 m
Colour:	Red, brown and beige
Hair type:	Thick
Foot length:	Up to 60 cm
Foot width:	Up to 20 cm
Body type:	Square shoulders, no neck and paddle-shaped hands
Sounds:	High-pitched cries and grunts

Early report

In 1884, the *British Colonist* newspaper reported an incident with a Sasquatch. The article said several men had found a "half-man, half-beast" asleep on railway tracks near the British Columbian town of Yale. They chased the creature and captured it.

After the article was published, a local man wrote that similar creatures had been seen fishing and hunting around his town of Lytton.

No one knows what happened to the captured creature, and many people consider the story a **hoax**. However, there have been many reported sightings of Sasquatch in this part of Canada ever since.

Naming Sasquatch

The word Sasquatch comes from the Salish word "sasq'ets", which means "wild man", or "hairy man". The Salish are **indigenous** people from North America's Pacific Northwest. Some think Sasquatch and Bigfoot are the same creature.

Modern hunters

From the 1920s to the 1950s, there were many more Sasquatch sightings in Canada. In the 1950s, two men dedicated their lives to finding the Sasquatch.

Rene Dahinden interviewed eye-witnesses and took hundreds of plaster casts of Sasquatch footprints. Dahinden died in 2001 after telling a close friend, "I've spent 40 years – and I didn't find it."

John Green also spent his life investigating the Sasquatch and wrote several books about the creature. He died in 2011, with plenty of information about Sasquatch sightings – but no Sasquatch.

Video footage

In 2011, climbers on British Columbia's Tantalus Mountain Range shot a stunning video of what they say was a Sasquatch. The footage shows a large, black figure in the distance, moving quickly across a snowy valley.

The valley is remote and people are seldom seen there. The figure in the video is tall and fast at walking on snow. The mountaineers swore it was the Sasquatch. However, so far, there is also nothing to prove the figure wasn't a person. The search goes on ...

Searching the science

Canadian scientist, Mark Collard, says every Sasquatch sighting should be investigated. There are plenty of records in British Columbia of eyewitness accounts, photographs of footprints, audio recordings and more. However, scientists need proof.

"Extraordinary claims require extraordinary evidence," Collard told Canadian TV. "At this point, the only strong evidence would be something direct, like **skeletal** remains or a cadaver (dead body) ... Until then, scientists will remain sceptical," Collard said.

Scientific samples

In 2012, scientists from the UK and Switzerland looked at hair samples said to be from the Yeti, Bigfoot, Sasquatch, or similar creatures. However, the samples turned out to belong to bears, horses, porcupines and sheep.

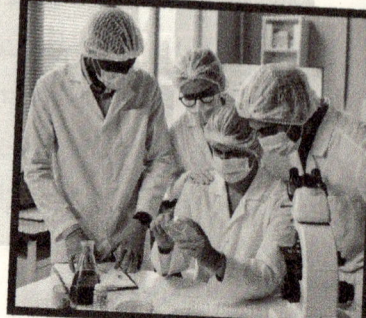

Eyewitness account

In 1955, climber William Roe had a Sasquatch encounter in British Columbia's Mica Mountain. This is his account:

" My first impression was of a huge man ... Its broad frame was straight from shoulder to hip. Its arms were much thicker than a man's arms, and longer, reaching almost to its knees. Its feet were broader proportionately than a man's ... But the hair that covered it ... made it resemble an animal as much as a human. "

The Sasquatch sighting in Silverton turned out to be a false alarm. The tracks had been made by a moose. I was not too disappointed, however, as I heard there had been another Bigfoot sighting in nearby Alaska, in the United States.

I arrived here in Alaska, where massive footprints have been found on a frozen lake. The park **ranger** showed me photos. He thinks the tracks belong to a wolf, but they look too big.

So now I've spent several hours trekking to the lake. I used my foldable shovel to build an igloo from blocks of snow. Inside, I've carved an ice bench to sit on, and a slit that I can peer out of. Now I am sitting here, watching and waiting.

BIGFOOT

Height:	1.8–3 m
Colour:	Brown, red and black
Hair type:	Shaggy
Foot length:	35–60 cm
Foot width:	Up to 25 cm
Body type:	Bulky, stocky, with a big, barrel chest
Sounds:	Howls, growls and high-pitched whistles

Expert opinion: Jane Goodall

Jane Goodall is a famous biologist who spent decades studying gorillas in Africa. She believes Bigfoot exists.

"I've met people who swear they've seen Bigfoot. I think the interesting thing is on every single continent there is an equivalent of Bigfoot or Sasquatch," Goodall says.

Bigfoot begins

The modern Bigfoot legend began in 1958, with an article in Californian newspaper, *The Humboldt Times*. The headline read, "Giant footprints puzzle residents along Trinity River."

The footprints had been found by **loggers** who called the creature that made them "Bigfoot". The name stuck.

The loggers made a plaster cast of a footprint. It was 45 cm long and 17 cm wide. News of the "Bigfoot" quickly spread. However, one of the loggers later admitted they had made the footprint themselves. The story had been a hoax!

Bigfoot attack

In 1962, Robert Hatfield reported a Bigfoot attack in Fort Bragg, California. It happened outside his family cabin.

"It was much, much bigger than a bear. It was covered with fur, with a flat, hairless face and perfectly round eyes," Hatfield said.

Hatfield raced to get inside, but the creature tried to stop him from closing the door. After it left, he found a 27 cm dirty handprint on the door and a 40 cm footprint below it.

It has been a frustrating few days. There has not been any sign of Bigfoot.

However, I have just been sent this text message:

"Ucumar sighting in the Andes Mountains!"

So, I have decided to pack up and chase this lead!

South America

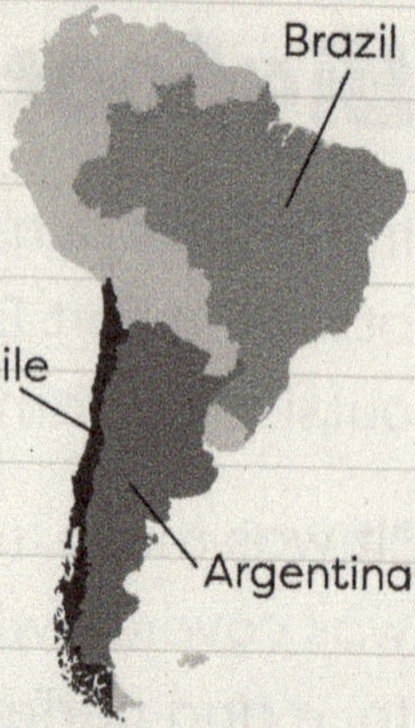

I'm on a flight to the Andes Mountains between Chile and Argentina, where the Ucumar has been seen. But we've hit a lightning storm. The plane is getting tossed around and I am finding it hard to write. I hope we will land safely!

UCUMAR

Height:	1.6–2.4 m
Colour:	Brown or black
Hair type:	Furry with a long beard
Foot length:	30–60 cm
Foot width:	Up to 20 cm
Body type:	Big, bulky with red eyes
Sounds:	Eerie calls at night

Call of the wild

In 1956, footprints 43 cm long were discovered in the Andes mountains. The next year, similar tracks were found nearby in Salta, Argentina. Local people said they could hear eerie calls at night, coming from the mountains. The calls made a "Uhu, uhu, uhu" sound.

Bathing beast

The Ucumar is thought to live in Argentina and Chile. Eyewitnesses say it looks like a bear crossed with a big man. It has huge hands, a long beard, a narrow forehead, and likes bathing in rivers. It is reported to eat cabbages and has been known to scream at cows and chickens.

In 1958, campers near Santiago, Chile, reported being visited by the Ucumar. They said it looked like "an enormous man covered with hair". Around the same time, giant footprints were found in the area. These led high up into the mountains. However, the Ucumar could not be found.

Eyewitness account

In 2022, a Chilean farmer reported seeing the Ucumar one night. This is his account:

> I heard that the dogs were barking and charging towards the field ... I grabbed my **flashlight** and went to look. The dogs were scared and came right back. When I shone my light, I was completely terrified because there was this thing, it was like a big, hairy, dark-coloured gorilla ... I saw his red eyes. Then, he went into the bush.

I've just learned that the plane cannot land in this storm and we have to fly to Brazil. So, I'm going to skip the Ucumar and instead search for the Mapinguari. You have to be flexible when Yeti hunting!

I'm now in the Brazilian rainforest by the Amazon River. I was picked up at the airport and driven here by a local Mapinguari hunter. She is following up on a recent sighting, and has brought me along.

We are watching the rainforest from a **camouflaged** platform in the trees. Who knows what we'll see below?

MAPINGUARI

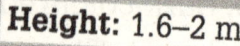

Height:	1.6–2 m
Colour:	Brown or red
Hair type:	Gorilla-like
Foot length:	30–40 cm
Foot width:	Up to 25 cm
Body type:	Square-shouldered with a second mouth on its stomach
Sounds:	Thundering roar

Horrible cries

The Mapinguari has often been heard, rather than seen. Its cry is said to be "horrible, deafening and inhuman". Those who claim to have caught a glimpse of the Mapinguari say it is a terrifying sight. This is because it has a second mouth situated on its stomach. It is also reported to stink like sour, rotting cabbages.

Mapinguari hair samples have been analysed by a local scientist, Dr David Oren. He found some of the hair belonged to an agouti – a type of guinea pig. Oren said he thought the Mapinguari was probably some kind of a sloth.

We've been in our tree-top lookout for three days and it has not stopped raining! There's been no sign of the Mapinguari. I have to admit that my spirits have been dampened. I'm off to somewhere dry: Africa.

Africa

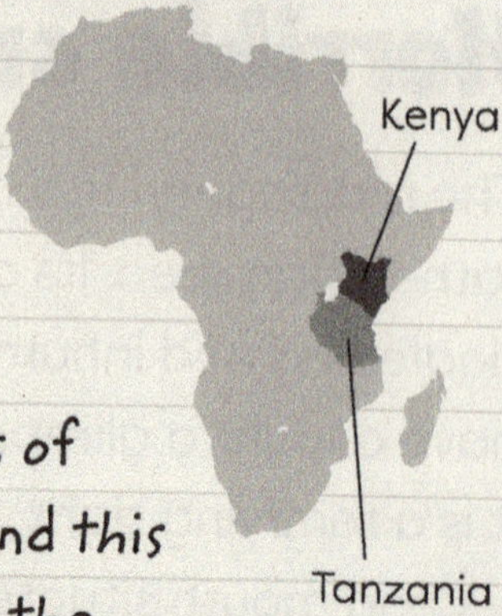

I'm now staying with the tribal Nandi people of Kenya. For centuries, there have been sightings of the Chemosit (Yeti) around this highland village. Some of the village hunters are taking me out tonight to search for it.

Kenya

Tanzania

CHEMOSIT

Height:	1.5–2 m
Colour:	Brown or beige
Hair type:	Shaggy
Foot length:	14–50 cm
Foot width:	Up to 15 cm
Body type:	Thick, stocky body, pointed snout, small ears
Sounds:	Hyena-type cry, moaning call

Bear or hyena?

The Nandi people say the Chemosit is a cross between a bear and a hyena. It can run on all fours and also walk upright. In 1913, a Chemosit was seen wandering around Kenya's Magadi railway station. It was said to jump out of trees and attack people.

We searched for the Chemosit under a full moon. The hunters tried to scare me by saying it loves eating human brains. Sadly, the hunters admitted that no one has seen a Chemosit for years.

They have suggested that instead I should search for the Ngoloko creature in the Yaeda Valley, Tanzania. They are going to help me get there.

Hairless face

The Ngoloko is known as the Sasquatch of East Africa. Tall, terrible smelling, and covered in thick hair, the Ngoloko has rarely been seen. However, in 1917, a tribesman said he was stalked by an Ngoloko. He and his friends shot it with an arrow, and examined it while it lay wounded.

The Ngoloko was said to be an odd sight. It had long hair, a hairless face and big, flapping ears like an elephant. Its eyes, nose and teeth were large, but its mouth was small. Some of its fingers and toes were clawed.

Unfortunately, the wounded Ngoloko died and was not studied further.

NGOLOKO

Height:	1.8–2.4 m
Colour:	Grey
Hair type:	Thick, long hair, especially on its head
Foot length:	20–50 cm
Foot width:	Up to 25 cm
Body type:	Hairless face, huge ears, big nose and teeth
Sounds:	High-pitched cry, scarier than a gorilla's

Ngoloko in folklore

According to local folklore, the Ngoloko was once a friendly spirit. But, one day it did something wrong and was sent away. Afterwards, the Ngoloko lived alone in swamps. It is said to have survived by drinking milk and blood.

Eyewitness account

Writer John Elliot said he saw Ngoloko tracks in 1917. He could tell the tracks came from something weighing twice as much as a human man. The track was definitely not made by a hoofed animal, but one with a claw.

It has taken days to get to the Yaeda Valley. Here, two Hadza tribesmen helped me set up camp near the Yaeda River.

Recently, large, unexplained footprints were found on the riverbank. Terrifying, high-pitched cries have been heard here at night.

As dusk fell, night-time creatures started making croaks, chirps and whistles. I realised I was being watched. Standing beside a **baobab** tree was a tall, dark figure.

It was much bigger than a human. I felt its eyes on me as I reached for my camera ...

But suddenly, there was a mighty splash from the river. A crocodile grabbed a **wildebeest** in its jaws. It was rolling the wildebeest in the river to drown it.

A terrible cry came from by the baobab tree. I caught a glimpse of the figure running. And just like that, it was gone.

Europe

Scotland

Wales

The search goes on! Now, I'm in the highlands of Scotland. I have pitched my camp in the Cairngorm mountains. The mountain range is reportedly home to the terrifying creature Am Fear Liath Mor, commonly called the Big Grey Man.

Known as the Scottish Yeti, the Big Grey Man strikes fear into the hearts of all who encounter it. I must be extra careful.

BIG GREY MAN

Height:	2–3 m
Colour:	Grey, brown
Hair type:	Short, thick
Foot length:	30–50 cm
Foot width:	Up to 35 cm
Body type:	Large head, slim hips, pointy ears
Sounds:	High-pitched singing call

Eyewitness account

In 1891, Professor Norman Collie was walking in the Cairngorms when he realised he was being followed. This is his account:

> I was returning from the cairn on the summit in a mist when I began to think I heard something else than merely the noise of my own footsteps. For every few steps I took, I heard a crunch, and then another crunch, as if someone was walking after me ... I listened and heard it again, but could see nothing in the mist. As I walked on, and the eerie crunch, crunch sounded behind me, I was seized with terror and took to my heels, staggering blindly among the boulders for four or five miles nearly down.

Welsh or Scottish?

In the Snowdonia region of Wales, there have been reports of a Big Grey Man called Brenin Llwyd. It is also said to strike a feeling of dread into climbers. Could it be the same creature?

In the 20th century, there were more encounters with the Big Grey Man in the Cairngorms. They include:

1920s: Climber Tom Crowley heard footsteps and turned to see a giant figure behind him. Crowley noticed the figure had large, bird-like claws on its feet.

1943: Mountaineer Alexander Tewnion was on a 10-day climb when a strange figure charged at him. He shot at it with his pistol, before running down the mountain.

1945: Rescue climber Peter Densham heard strange noises and felt pressure around his neck. He wriggled away and escaped unharmed.

I felt uneasy from the moment I set up my tent. It was still and silent, with a soupy mist hanging over everything. It was hard not to feel a sense of dread.

Out of nowhere, I heard a crunch. And another. It sounded as if someone, or something, was walking towards me. I grabbed my camera and stood up, not knowing where to point it. The crunch, crunch, crunch became louder. Then, there was a terrifying, high-pitched sound.

Suddenly, a large figure loomed up before me. I fell backwards, but picked myself up and ran. Behind me, I could hear the crunching footsteps getting closer. I fell again, and tumbled down a bank. I slipped many metres and landed on spongy moss below.

There is no mist down here and nothing has followed me. I am safe, but my camera has been smashed, so there is no evidence of the encounter!

Asia

After my scare in Scotland I wondered if I should call off the search. The experience shook me up. But with my camera ruined, I still don't have proof a Yeti exists. I have therefore decided to continue.

I have bought a new camera and am heading for Asia. It is China's Huebi Province that I have set my sights on next. Many Yeren have been reported in the Shennongjia National Nature Reserve there.

Himalayas
China and Huebui Province

YEREN

Height:	2–3 m
Colour:	Red-brown
Hair type:	Thick, wavy
Foot length:	30–40 cm
Foot width:	Up to 20 cm
Body type:	Flat face, large nose
Sounds:	Yelling call and loud laugh

Wild man

There have been stories about the Yeren for many centuries in China. The creature is described as strong, savage, and able to move at great speed through forests and mountain ranges.

Yeren means "wild man" in Chinese, and the Yeren has a reputation for attacking people and raiding villages for food. Many people have dedicated their lives to hunting and killing the Yeren. No one has been successful so far.

Eyewitness account

In 1980, a villager in Shennongjia reported seeing a Yeren while collecting herbs. She said the Yeren was:

> about seven feet (2.1 m) tall, with reddish fur and long swinging arms.

In books

In his 853 CE book about Chinese legends, author Duan Chengshi described the Yeren in this way:

"Its shape is like that of an ape. It uses human speech, but it sounds like a bird ... legend has it that its heels face backwards ... hunters say that it has no knees."

Science steps in

After reports of the Yeren increased in the 1970s, a government expedition began. A search party of scientists, soldiers and photographers set out into the Shennongjia nature reserve. But they found little evidence of the Yeren. Some scientists think the Yeren is probably a bear or an orangutan.

During my stay in Shennongjia, I've heard a lot of stories about the Yeren. Some people have shown me samples of Yeren hair. But scientists say the hair is not genuine.

I've decided to venture north to the Himalayas in search of the Yeti, or Abominable Snowman, as it is sometimes called.

The Yeren Gateway arch is an enormous statue of a Yeren and its young. Situated at the entrance of Shennongjia National Nature Reserve, the statue indicates the start of 'Yeren country'.

39

I have reached Nepal and am determined to pick up the Yeti trail. I trek through the mountains towards the village of Khumjung. Here, locals say the Yeti has been spotted several times recently in neighbouring Tibet. Off I go!

YETI

Height:	2–3.5 m
Colour:	White, grey, sometimes reddish-brown
Hair type:	Shaggy
Foot length:	35–45 cm
Foot width:	Up to 35 cm
Body type:	Hairless face, large, sharp teeth
Sounds:	Grunts, whistles and howls

Himalayan folklore

The Yeti has lived for a long time in Himalayan folklore. Locals say a Yeti roams the mountains, feeds on **yaks** and bathes in hot-water springs. Western interest in the Yeti increased during attempts to climb Mount Everest.

Edmund Hillary, one of the first two men to climb Everest, led an expedition to find a Yeti in 1960. But despite seeing large footprints in the snow, and finding a supposed "Yeti **scalp**", the search came up empty-handed. All scientific expeditions since have also failed to find a Yeti.

Yeti scalp

The "Yeti scalp" discovered by Edmund Hillary was found in the home of a local woman in Khumjung Village. The scalp is said to be over 300 years old, and now stays locked in a glass box. However, it was examined by experts many years ago. They found the scalp had been made from the hide of an antelope.

Eyewitness account

In 1925, photographer N. A. Tombazi said he saw a Yeti near the Himalayan Zemu Glacier. This is how he described it:

> Unquestionably, the figure in outline was exactly like a human being, walking upright and stopping occasionally to pull at some dwarf rhododendrons bushes. It showed up dark against the snow, and as far as I could make out, wore no clothes.

Expert opinion: David Attenborough

David Attenborough is a famous broadcaster and biologist who believes the Yeti exists. He said:

"I believe the Abominable Snowman may be real ... If you have walked the Himalayas, there are these immense rhododendron forests that go on for hundreds of square miles which could hold the Yeti."

A Yeti sample

In 2017, university biologists examined samples of teeth, hair, bone and faeces said to be from a Yeti. The results showed that most of the samples came from brown or black bears. However, Yeti believers refused to be disappointed. Instead, they said the results simply showed that the Yeti has some bear genes.

Footprint finding

In 2019, the Indian army claimed to have found Yeti footprints in the Himalayas. However, the footprints were in a line, rather than side-by-side, like human footprints. They were dismissed as fakes.

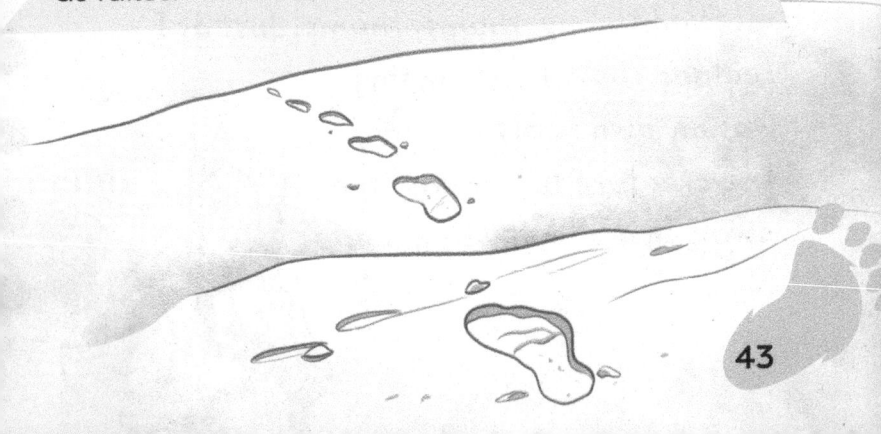

I have never been lost in Tibet until today. I sat on a mossy boulder to study my map but I haven't been able to pinpoint my location. I folded up my map and sat watching the dwindling light above the trees, knowing it would soon be dark.

Then, suddenly, something tall stepped silently into the space between me and the bushes. At first, I thought it was a yak. But slowly as my eyes focused, I saw that the creature was tall, with small eyes and a large round head. At that moment, everything stood still — even time seemed to slow down. The birds fell silent.

I heard the creature's breathing and a muffled thump, thump, thump. Just as I realised that the thumping was my own heart beating, the creature turned and sped away. In a blur, it was gone.

44

I was too slow to film the moment with my camera. But I am overjoyed. After so many years, I have proven what I knew as a child. The creatures I saw both back then and again today were not bears, or apes. They were Yetis. And my search to find more of these creatures will continue!

Yeti near you?

There are estimated to be around 1.8 million plants and animal species on Earth. Every year, thousands of species are discovered. Sadly, hundreds and perhaps thousands become **extinct** each year, mainly because of climate change.

It is possible, therefore, that the Yeti once existed and has now fallen into extinction. However, nobody knows for sure. There may be a Yeti out in the wild, somewhere near you!

Glossary

baobab	a large type of tree native to Africa
camouflaged	hidden or disguised
contact	a friend or local guide
encounter	to come face-to-face with something
extinct	die out
flashlight	torch
hoax	something fake which is pretending to be real
indigenous	people who originally lived and may continue to live in a particular country or region
loggers	forest workers who chop down trees
ranger	a special worker that protects a forest and its wildlife
scalp	the top part of the skull that has hair and skin
skeletal	the bones that belong to a skeleton
wildebeest	an African antelope
yaks	long-haired ox found in Tibet and parts of central Asia

Index

Abominable Snowman 3, 5, 39, 40-45

Am Fear Liath Mor 3, 32-35

Argentina 3, 20-22

Bigfoot 3, 5, 6, 11, 16-19

Brazil 3, 23-25

Brenin Llwyd 3, 33

Canada 3, 10-16

Chemosit 3, 26-27

Chile 3, 20-23

climate change 8, 45

China 3, 36-39

footprints 4, 6, 10, 12, 14, 16, 18, 19, 21, 30, 41, 43

Himalayas 6, 39, 41-43

Kenya 3, 26-27

Mapinguari 2, 23-25

Nepal 3, 40

Ngoloko 3, 27-31

Sasquatch 3, 5, 6, 10-16, 28

science and scientists 2, 14, 25, 38, 39

Scotland 3, 32-35. 36

Tanzania 3, 27-31

Tibet 3, 40, 44

Ucumar 3, 20-23

USA 3, 16-19

Wales 3, 33

Yeren 3, 36-39

Yeti 3, 4-5, 6-9, 14, 23, 26, 32, 36, 39, 40-45

Now answer the questions ...

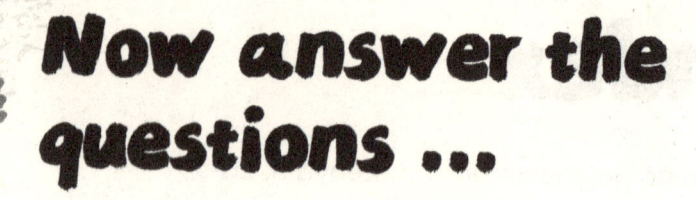

1 Give the meaning for the word 'logger' on page 18.

2 How many different names are there for the Yeti?

3 What type of vegetable did a Mapinguari smell like?

4 The Ngoloko had flapping ears like which animal?

5 Why did the Sasquatch sighting on page 16 turn out to be a false alarm?

6 Why is some of the book in a journal format and some in fact boxes?

7 Where did men from the British Columbian town of Yale say they found a Sasquatch?

8 Which is your favourite type of Yeti mentioned in this book? Why?